Wild Chai

Wild Chai

Poetry by
Cheriese Françoise Anderson

Copyright © 2020 Cheriese Françoise Anderson

The right of Cheriese Anderson to be identified as the Author of the Work has been asserted by her in accordance with the Copyright, Designs and Patents Act 1988

All images Copyright © Camilla French Photography

Images may not be used nor duplicated without written permission from aforementioned photographer

No duplication of this publication is permitted unless by Author of the Work Cheriese Anderson and / or with written permission from aforementioned Author.

Every effort has been made to comply with copyright legislation however Author is more than happy to rectify any oversights as quickly as possible should there be any.

Poem "Wearing the ocean" inspired by a prompt by Silver Leaf Poetry

ISBN: 978-0-6489630-0-4 (Pbk)
978-0-6489630-1-1 (e-Book)

A catalogue record for this book is available from the National Library of Australia

Dedicated to your heart from hers...

she had grown tired
of waiting
for them to tell her
all the words
she needed to hear
and so
she wrote them
herself....

She spent the secret hours

between midnight and dawn

writing love letters to her own heart

she poured out all the words of adoration she knew

sprawling them across the pages

line after line

the very same words

she had always spent on others

only now

they were meant

just for her....

You can feel it
she is not new here
there's something in
her mood
her shallow gaze
that hides the stories
of years untold
head in coloured clouds
and daydreams
yet grounded in the clay
of earth from which she came
her foundation is deep seated
and her aura sings
old soul...

she is in love
with the hand sewn stitch
along the edge of a soft linen sheet
she's like a fine blend
of smooth almond milk and wild chai
and wears sweet and salty grains
of pink sand and coconut sugar
on her skin
like diamonds
sweet nectar on her lips lingers
on the hem of every word she speaks
she will take nothing from you
that you aren't willing to give
yet she scatters wishes into the wind
under a twilight moon
that one day
she might be seen
she might be loved
in the same way
she loves that hand sewn stitch
along the edge
of a soft linen sheet

Some days
all she wanted
was to melt
into that silence
that fills the space
between thoughts
just to stay there
a little while
in hope that the quiet
might leak through
the threads of consciousness
you see
sometimes the soul aches
with a yearning
to release
in such a way
that no words
can quite articulate
so it's there
in that silent void
between thoughts
she waits
she listens
she rests

Evening draws in
and the sun lays gently
it's last kiss of the day
upon her praising earth
and with tender tips
of tired fingers
she grazes blissful air
with the affection
of one lover
to another
and as the heat
draws sweat
from the soft skin
of her neck
just like the moon
pulls willing tides
as it may
she closes her eyes
and lets the magic
of twilight paint her mind
with lines of love
that fall straight from
the burning evening sky
and she breathes in
that warmth so deep
and sings it out
in poetry

And if she were to burst
would stardust scatter
right from her seams
would the golden
of her soul fill eyes
with treasure they'd not seen
would all the untapped wonder
inside her skin
finally spill free
would the world
be that much brighter
if she just let her spirit be...

What light you harbour inside your skin
won't you let your spirit be
for this world it needs your magic
won't you let yourself be free

It's as though
she walks around
with her forget me not
kind of soul
scattering leaves
of wild berry
and rose behind her
as you drink her down
the scent of her
entwining
with yours
and the longer you spend
with her infused
in your waters
the harder it is
to wash away
her stain
the thing is
you won't notice
as it happens
but when you do
you won't even mind...

She has fallen
too far in love
with her own skin
to wear somebody else's
she's been down
that road before
of bending bones and
wearing strangers clothes
for the sake of
someone else's mould
and she won't go back
down that road
for you
she is too far in love
with her own soul

She met each morning

breathless

with the anticipation of the day

flooding her veins

and tingling in the tips

of her fingers

electrified...

it was inescapable

the exhilaration

sparked

in her soul

fuelling the flames of infatuation

for seeking everything

that made her feel

anything

but ordinary

There she waits
in the in between
there she counts
endless nothings
in the countless threads
of the jute rug
collecting dust
as her mind
collects daydreams
in these passing hours
There she waits
In the in between
she forgets
the desperation
of the usual scramble
for more hours
to do more things
more things
that don't mean much
to our hearts at all
taking sips of seconds
drinking them down
slowly
into minutes
trickling into hours
into days
tasting the entirety
and the distinct sweetness
all at once
there she waits
in the in between
waiting for nothing
at all

The layers of her

each more delicate than the last

she is layered

she is more

than one kind of thing

inside that gentle frame

a water colour painting

her skittish hues blurring through

until there is hardly distinction at all

to the naked eye

the eye that doesn't care to see

to take the time

in the quiet corner

of a dimly sun touched room

to explore her fusion

learning all her shades

by name

and she won't

stay this way

any longer than

need be

she won't be bound

to but one version

of herself

and she won't bend

or break to suit

the expectations

of this world

for she is

after all

an ever changing soul

always ready

always waiting

for her next dance

Don't hesitate
to love her
like something unsure
sipping gingerly as though
you've been forced
to drink her down
she's the kind of love
that begs to be
swallowed whole
she won't let you
take her warmth for granted
because it's yours
if you know how to hold it
but if you can't
tend to her heart
and keep her wild sparks alight
then maybe
you aren't the one
to fall into the fire with her
and she won't have her love
any other way
so don't leave her too long
in the cold of your shoulder
take her in
and let her consume you
like flames licking at
the coldest corners
of your heart
and setting fire
to all you thought
you knew about love
before her....

In her hands
she held the hearts
of those
who had broken hers
and over them
she wept
tears of letting go
and with them fell
the weight she'd carried
the weight of another's sin
her burden no more
she let them flow
washing her wounds
and although
they would leave a scar
she would not resent
their presence on her skin
marked like pages
of her story
the ones she would read over
they would remind her
of the perils
of being reckless
with her love
but also of the healing
in her own hands

And her greatest

feat of all

her death defying act

of hurtling

head first and blindly

into her wild

without a care

in the world

as to who

if anyone at all

might catch her

because the freedom

from the life

slowly taking her

piece by piece

was the closest thing

to being alive

she had ever felt

she relishes in the quiet

of the silent breeze

breathing through

her shattered windows

she is still

as her glass makes room

for those morning rays of sun

whispering to her warm secrets

of the night passed

She creates....

with every move she makes

she manifests

with every breath drawn

she spins wonder

from her mind

and beauty

with her hands

like it was always

meant to be done

it is her passion

and her conviction

recognising each day

for the gift

that it is

for even the stillest of hours

are soaked with inspiration

and for the life of her

she will not let

not a single drop

go to waste

and so she goes
further along
away from their voices
into the quiet
with only the chatter
of rocks and pebbles
scattering
at her bare feet
she could never quite say
how she always knew
the perfect pavement
lined with lush green
and sunlight
was never meant
for her
and while it may scream uncertainty
this quiet shadowed path
it whispers carry on
yes it's quiet
and she can only see
so far ahead
but one tender step
at a time
she takes
like a slow brew
of ginger and lemon tea
she bubbles slow
with no noise to follow
nothing to follow at all
but as her bare feet
trail through the cocoa dirt
she traces shapes
of waves and spirals
with her toes
twirling in the dust
she lets it fly
eyes closed
as it settles
on her face
adorning her
in the markings
of the road
less travelled.

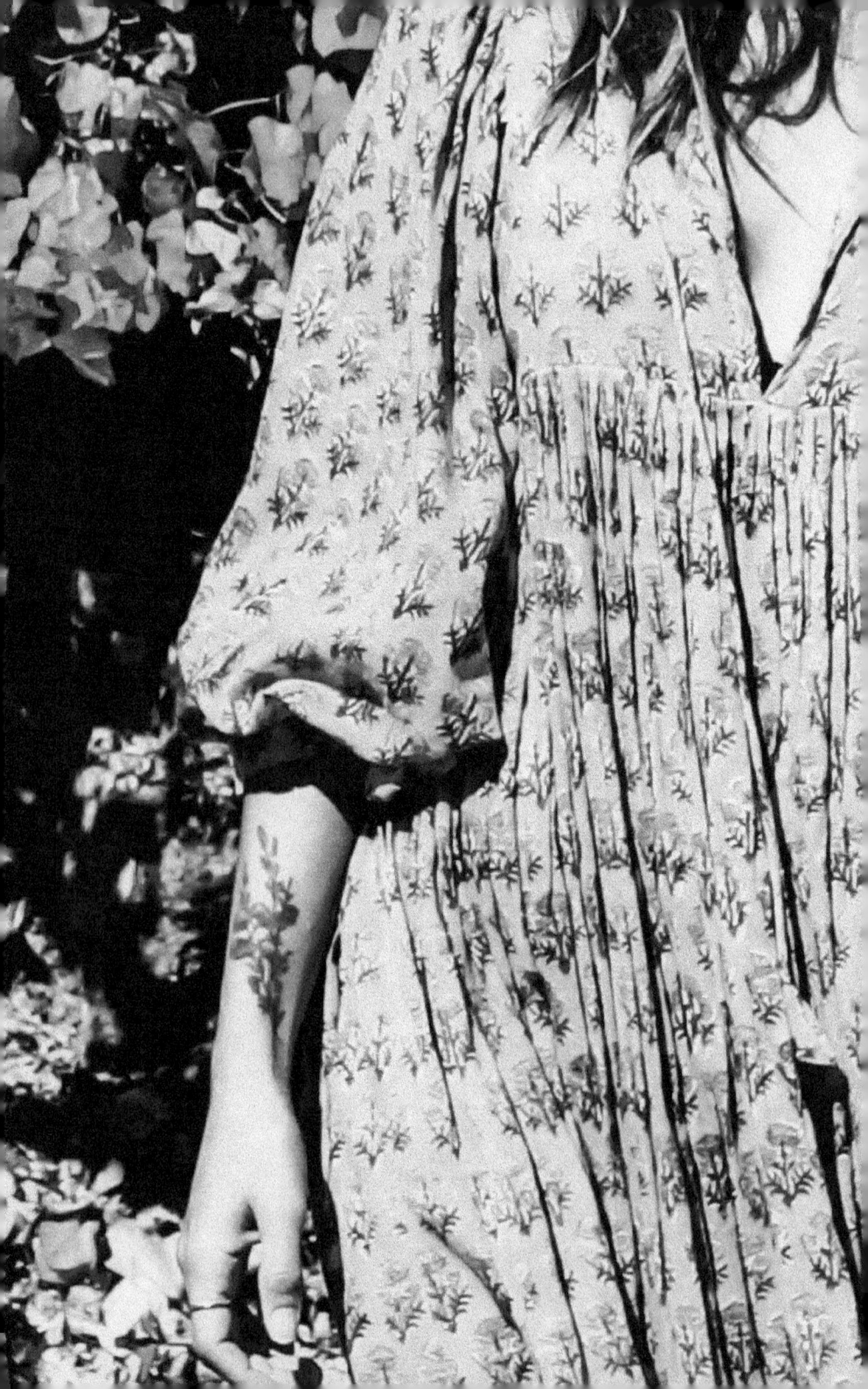

and she would never

be so careless

again

as to place something

so precious

as her heart

into dirty hands

with quick fingers

for even though

she understood

that her own

were far from clean

her nails stained

with blood

and laced with soil

from her own

deeply set grave

at least she knew

where they had been

I've cast wishes
on a flimsy star or two
for the things
I was told
held the feeling
that I sought
and it's the most
tempting thing
I know
to fall head over heels
for the beauty
of the mask
but the vacant face
beyond it
cares little for the inhale
undervalues the pause
and won't allow you
the room you need
to exhale
haven't you heard
it all before
the promise of gold
to fill the holes
the ones that grow
day after day
inside your suffocating soul
but don't you know
your soul is made
not of a gold
that can be sold
and all you need
to be complete
lies waiting in
your empty palm
I know you'll say
this but a dream
is far too simple
to be true
but atleast believe
the stories
of the wildflower
who blooms
in spite of where
she finds herself
in this beautiful
cruel world

the revelation

it came

on yet another night

alone with her

staring back at me

with desperate eyes

as I tore flesh

from her tired bones

piercing her skin

with the sharpest edges

of my mind

I told her how

I loathed her

every curve

and mark

and line

so unforgiving

salting every wound

that I could find

it came

as the moon seduced

the tears

right from my

hopeless eyes

and as they fell

with them away

all of their blind lies

and there she was

I saw her

as though

it were for the first time

for all the things

my body was

and all

I'd put her through

she carried me

she carried on

both for and

in spite of me

she carries me

she carries on

both one with

and apart from me

she was my home

I wrapped my arms

around her

and let our tears fall

til they dried

and on my knees

begged her forgiveness

and forgiveness came

that night...

Don't be so timid
tenderly sipping slow
from the glass
you've been cradling
in clammy palms
unsure for too long
as though somehow
it doesn't really
belong to you
or maybe it might burn
going down
but I'm begging you
not to let that fear
hold you back
from drowning yourself
in that steaming elixir
of self love
that is rightfully
yours
and yours alone
take it all down
drench yourself in
that not so guilty pleasure
draw it in deep
like air filling your lungs
with every breath
get caught up
in that rush
of falling deeper
in sickly sweet love
with every last drop
of your own mind
body and soul

...and you can't help

but fall in love

with all her

wildflower ways

collect her petals

dark and light

and let her sweetness

soften your heart

while her wonder

keeps your eyes

filled with

stars

Silver wind chimes
throw light like stars
across my bedroom walls
while the breeze
stained with eucalyptus
breathes through
and I watch
the last of blue
for the days sky
as it whispers away
calling the golden
evening sun
to follow too
and as night begins
to roll slowly in
and shadows cast
over my skin
and the curlews croon
their lovesick serenade
the hum of twilight
plays along
like some forgotten
sacred song
while weeping willows
murmur their sweet melody
then my dear moon
begins to rise
pouring her light
into my eyes
does she know
that I've been waiting
all day long
for the hush
that she lays down
like curtains drawing
on the crowd
there's something in her mood
that lulls this restless soul
so every day
at the same time
inside this peace
she helps me find
I fall deeper
into my love
for the sound
of twilight

and the stars
they dwelled
in the flecks
of her eyes
so she
could see light
in the darkest
of nights...

To the moon and back
is nice my love
but why should we stop there
when there's a galaxy beyond us
it calls us to let go
it begs to ignite the heart
that dares to burn
I won't settle for the distant light
of fading constellations
and lukewarm nights
without a flame to kindle
I seek so much more my dear
by now you know this well
it's that otherworldly love I want
let's fall under its spell
for I'm a stardust kind of soul
with a heart among the clouds
and I will shoot for what they won't
why can't the endless skies be ours
I don't need a fickle love
that leaves at sight of morning sun
lets smoulder slow and steady
through the day
and set the night alight
adore me
love
like the stars adore the moon
and how the moon adores the sun
untouched by hands of time
for I won't love like falling stars
bright for a while
magic a moment
beautiful for one breath
I'm a burn forever lover
burn with me....

Weary
frail
you move through the days
and accept their toll
still in the night
though not all the way through
you stir almost like clockwork
every hour
on the hour
welcoming the new day
with the same fatigue
as the one before
cracks on your surface
spread like fractured glass
they spill over the hills and valleys
like a map to destinations
already travelled
you groan with every drawn in wind
and sigh with each release
and yet in spite of your tire
you are soft
so indescribably soft
delicate
like tender petals and silk
make up your lining
and your warmth
always blissfully warm
like a sip of spicy chai
trickling mellow comfort
down the throat
so forgiving you are
of that which has afflicted you
you do not waver
relentlessly
you carry on
moving through each day
and while you may be weary
frail
you are in your entirety
the embodiment
of strength and life itself

*It seems as though
she might
be someone else
entirely
between the hours
of 3am and dawn
someone who
can spin a line
turning darkness
into sparks of light
sprawled across
stone paper pages
and when she wakes
she finds the words
and can't be sure
these thoughts are hers
now shes convinced
within herself
these stories just might
belong to the moon*

Create me

I want to see
how you would breathe
me to life
paint me pretty
with your thoughts
with all the colours
of your heart
draw for me
the flowers you see
blooming
from the soles
of my feet
sing me true
with a voice unbridled
and let me hear
my words fall
from your mouth
mould me
into a pear shaped vase
to be filled
with each rise
of the sun
and emptied once more
under the guidance
of the stars
create me
for I am desperate
to be bought
to life

She's a
too many thoughts in her sea
kind of girl
her sweet shallows
only go so far
before she is pulled back in
by the raging depths
of a mind
that knows
no rest

Come inside sunshine
there isn't much here left to hide
you see the curtains that once hung here
have been stripped away tonight
notice the way the light does fall
across the dusty length of floor
can you see the faded colours
and the cracks along the walls
broken glass gleams in the corners
stained with blood both new and old
there are embers that still smoulder
from the pile of lies I've told
you might hear the faintest whisper
of the girl I used to be
the one who hid here in the shadows
of the parts of me unseen
she hung the curtains
swept the dust
painted the cracks
of broken trust
and at the sight of her heart broken
scattered like glass over the floor
she tried to force it back together
but I pulled it apart once more
you see I like the way the sunlight
feels against my fractured core
and I won't cut my hands again
trying to hide it from you all
so I say welcome to my soul
I know it's different from before
when who I used to be lived here
but she doesn't anymore

And every day would not be
stories of sweet tea
under painted skies
or lullabies of afternoon breeze
and the way the light dances
between leaves
for some days
felt as though
the worlds whole weight
rested
in the space between
behind her eyes
and the forefront of
her mind
and these days that felt
so heavy
yet were so empty
all at once
they were the ones
she seldom wrote about
until today....

*Today is heavy
for no reason at all
but I feel my bones tremble
and splinter under its weight
and the tire
overwhelms me
I feel it even before
I open my eyes
and days like this
have such a way
of drawing my insecurities
right out into the light
it's days like this
I spend the hours
longing for the lull
of night
when I can send this day
back on my dreams
in hope the next
will be more
like the one before*

And when it broke
my heart
it scattered into countless pieces
of a thousand colours
shards of dreams once held
and one by one
they fall
back together
into an ever changing
chaotic kaleidoscope
so much more beautiful
than it used to be...

Some days weighed heavier
than others
she wondered how
a souls burden
might be felt in the ether
when the spirits light is low
breath shallow
with a mood like
grey and black
fusing in the sky
swelling slow and steady
waiting

to

fall...

She has

but one room

in her heart

only a few steps down

her splintered hall

move slowly past

her shattered glass

until you reach

her humble door

with dust of sandalwood

and myrrh seeping out

from underneath

and if you care

to take the time

to breathe in deep

her gold within

then she will let you

make your home here

and she will make

you golden too

She collected pieces
of herself
like shells on the shore
choosing only
the prettiest colours
and shapes
to create a picture
in her mind
of what she was
or should be
until the moment
she realised
that every beautiful piece
of what she had come
to know
as her self
in one way or another
kept her mind tethered
to her suffering
and it would be only
in the relinquish
of every beautiful piece
she collected
along the way
every ideal
of what should be
that she clung to
only when this illusion
was let go
and acceptance
of just being
embraced
could the ties
to her suffering
be truly severed...

She's that's one place
you can come back to
anytime you need her calm
you close your eyes
and draw her in
deep and slow
slow and steady
and she'll let you take her
even when she's out of mind
she fuels your pulse
runs through your blood
breezing sweet
over your tongue
lose her in the rush
of racing hearts
beating out of time
only to find her once again
when you come back down
and she'll keep giving
while you keep taking
deep and slow
slow and steady
until the last of her
is gone

breath....

Delicate spine
arching freely
you give way
like bridges bowing
to make way
and make light
for their needs
you bend to them
without asking
to be lifted once again
but it's okay to
lay it down you know
the heavy
that you've been holding
you don't need it
to prove your worth
anymore
it will not serve you
to keep its weight
but it will surely
set you free
to let it go

In the hours
lit only by lunar hues
and flecks of
smouldering stars
straining through
an indigo sky
her mind becomes
something quite else
that it isn't quite
by day
there in the dark
her thoughts
transcend
flowing free
they slip out
of mind
and into pages
of words
stripped bare
of the veil
they wear
before the hours
of slumber awaken
and inhibition
rests....

Here she goes
stepping not so lightly
as before
as she chases her dreams
not like rainbows
but storms
thunder builds and shakes
the breath inside her chest
as wild winds
sweep her off dainty feet
and she is tumbling
further
away from all control
while falling
deeper
into the very core
of the life
she has been chasing

for so long

*Don't be afraid
to let go darling
for the chaos you fear
is dancing
to the most beautiful sound
of freedom....*

she has no bowls
of water
lined with crystals
to be cleansed
no intentions
to be set
no burdens or sage
to burn
what she has
is a mind silenced
as the moonlight
baths her skin
filling her eyes
and moving
her waters within
and it was
always something
she found
the hardest to describe
the way that milky light
looked right through
her frame of bones
drawing all she felt inside
out into the night

Just like
so many before her
she spent much of her life
searching
hungry to please
eager to prove
that she was worthy
of the love
she was convinced
would complete her
only to find
that what she sought
from them
she did not need
for it was the love
within her own heart
that her dear soul
was yearning for
and once she found it
even the stars
she so adored
could not compare
to the kind of light
she would become

she had never been weak
or even necessarily unsure
of who she was meant to be
she just lost her voice
somewhere between
his sweet nothings
and no where to lay
her head
but in the clouds
and in his shadow
she sang silent songs
of freedom
between her cries
tip toed softly
in his foot steps
between her falls
knowing one day
she would pull her voice
from somewhere well inside
and sing her freedom
in her own light
in her own step
in time she would
this she knew
and that hope
would lead her home

*We are the ones
with the bare feet
the messy minds
and starry eyes
the body and soul romantics
wearing our bleeding hearts
on our sleeves
we spill a thousand
abstract thoughts
with our ink and brush
like sparks
and let them fly
into the night
our countless colours
burning bright
with the full moon
we are the bohemians
the earth lovers
the art makers
the life creators
drawing our own paths
leaving stories
laced with stardust
and the ash
of worn conventions
in our wake*

Gold in her veins

she saw the cracks

of your heart broken

and reached between

fine china bones

for her own

shattered pieces

as though maybe

she could use them

to fill the holes

she saw in yours

she only wanted

to see you whole

with bloody hands

she gave you all

and she cried dry

her tears of gold

and left herself

an empty chest

a bleeding soul

her skin
was lined with the fibres
of gentle cotton gowns
and in them lingered
the soft fragrance
of hemp and thieves
rose and nag champa
wafted through
the rooms of her home
embedded in the fabric
of her bed sheets and pillows
and as each night fell
the sweet orange hues
of the salt lamp
glowing from the dusty shelf
filled the dark
I guess she had an affection
for things raw and unrefined
formed of the earth
from which she herself
and surrounded by them
she was reminded
that even on
the days she felt
most empty
she was as whole
as she needed to be

Her feet still tingled
like bubbles rising
crackling at the surface
of sweet lemonade
they'd itch
with any pair of shoes worn
too long
and while she missed
her dancing toes
left somewhere
between her youth
and the sting
of ankles twisted
stumbling across
the dark stage
of lessons learned
she would find her solace
in the gentle arch
of soles bare and worn
but wise

Wild

it flows through
her blood running hot
and fuels
her every heart beat
she is wild
but not in the way
you may think
she won't demand
your attention
with rooftop dances
or moonlight howls
but she'll shed her skin
bare her naked soul
and let you touch
her wounds
and though she might
steal away
to hide with her thoughts
once in a while
just let her be
for she'll come back to you
but you must let her
be free

She has this way
of pouring light
into a room
like a glass of sunshine
spills in with her
perhaps that was her magic
and it was not hers in vain
for she had known darkness
too well
too long
see one of two things can happen
to a person who has lived in the dark
they either carry that burden with them
seeking out the shadows
that have come to feel like home
or they become the embodiment
of light itself
and if you meet the latter
you will know

like a drifter twirling

her spray of wildflowers

carving the songs

of her name

in the trees

she may not know

where she is going

or even what she needs

but she will share

with you her stories

and she will let you

write your own

and where she can

her only hope is

to spark a little beauty

spread love like wildfire

and rekindle tepid hearts

as she goes

along her way....

It's now or never
I'm handing you this chance
to get your own palms dirty
your fingers bloody
reach as deep into my heart
as your mortal soul can take
and when you grasp my burning core
let the burn remind you once more
that I am the girl
who played with fire
I am the one
who danced with flames
and it was I
who rose from the embers
of the bed in which I laid
because it seems
you have forgotten
as the years
have turned lukewarm
but darling
I was never the one
you could leave in the corner
to reach for only
when you need warmth
I am the one
who will set fire
to the life
before your eyes

*Oh it's hard
for one so tender
and all feeling
with the kind of heart
that bleeds through lines
until they're blurred
sometimes it's easier
to let herself fall
willing and graceful
into those waiting arms
rather than let them
catch her first
eventually
inevitably
because they always do
but atleast this way
she gets to make believe
that the hold
it keeps on her
may be more
a secure embrace
in an old familiar place
and not the cold
lonely stranglehold
it really is*

- abandonment

She hesitates
to spell the words
that tell the secret things
that love
has made her feel
because to be honest
it's so much easier
not to let those memories
fall into the same box
as the word
but love it was
at least for a time
and that's the part
that hurts the most
because the wounds
are not so deep
when losing something
you never wanted
but they cut
to your core
when they're inflicted
in the name of something
you once thought
once hoped
would last forever

Sucked down the drain
of her memories once again
as she grasps at the edge
of her tolerance as though
if she happened to let go
she might just tumble
right back into them
without a pillow
to break her fall
and she'll feel it all again
like the blow
for the first time
tender on her flesh
like the bruise she guards
but can't help
scratching at herself
and she doesn't know why
she lets herself give in
to that begging ache
it's like it waits
for these nights
when weakness tends
to cloud the surface
of her better judgment
so tonight
she'll lean deep
into her wounds
and twist her weakened bones
she'll weigh on them
until the pressure
of her mood gives way
and she'll let it run through
until the sting
reaches through her core
and she will wonder
if perhaps there's something
in dwelling on misery passed
that she's not quite ready
to let go of yet...

Morning sun

breaks through

and comfort spills in

with the warmth

of golden rays

reminding her

of the way

we too bleed love

warmth and comfort

through our own darkness

when we allow ourselves

to be split apart

The road to her birth
laid with stories
of those before
yet to be unravelled
and while her ears
have never heard their voices
she feels it in her blood
the tongue of unheard songs
calling to her from somewhere past
stirring a craving in her soul
for all the memories
of places she has never been
the secrets of their tales
whisper through the water
flowing in her veins
wild as oceans crossed
well before gracing
the sunburnt soil
that finds itself
between her toes
the journey to her birth
is riddled with stories
the ones that paved the path
for every step made
by those before
leading up to her first breath
and while long gone they seem
and most forgotten
more with every fulfilled cycle
of her sweet moon
they live on through
dark cocoa eyes
and tea stained skin
and nostalgic wishes
for a time she's never seen

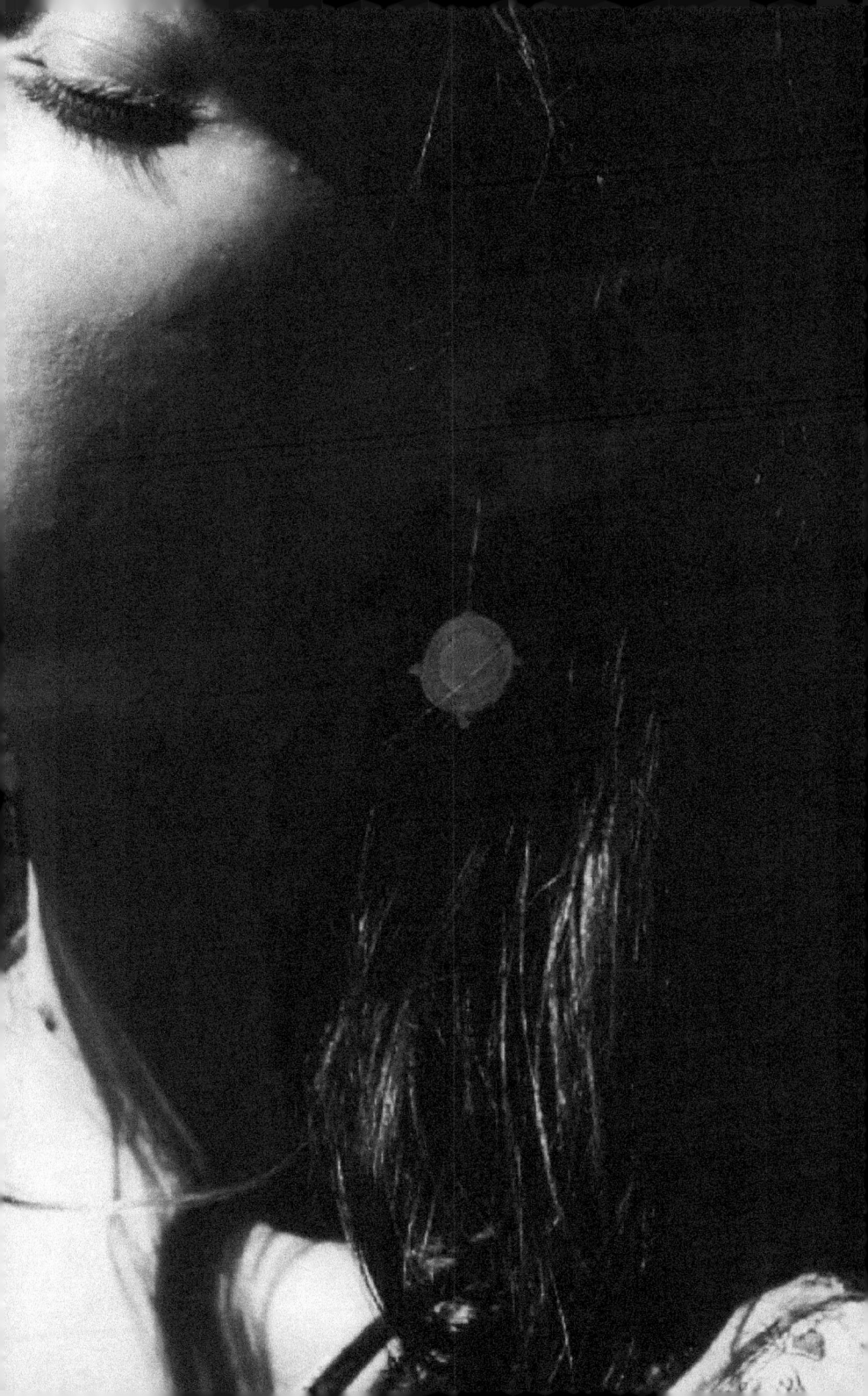

and she may wake
today
in rhythm
with every step
and beat of heart
with every breath
full of intention
and every thought
sweet affirmation
but somewhere along
the swoop of night
it swings away
from her once more
and when tomorrows
touch takes hold
as though the air
somehow turned cold
she finds herself
as out of stride
with her own breath
as erratic flutter
of butterfly wings
and just as delicate
drawing air as though
hard to swallow
her heart unsteady
like pitter patter
of falling rain...

Learn the lesson

lovely soul

breathe it in

through bleeding heart

and wounded spirit

let it blow

over frail bone

and tired mind

let it sit

at the bottom

of your gut

for a time

and then

when it has soaked

into the fabric

of your being

exhale

slow and gentle

keeping only

the truths you need

and letting go

of the pain you don't

Spending time
inside her own mind
was like a constant finding
of doors unopened
her colours swirled
in dying lines
dancing through
ink explosions
spattered over pages
painting pictures of her
rainbow coloured thoughts
there's something special about
that place
that belongs to her
and her alone

down here at the edge

of that salty moon lead water

serenity washes in

on foamy drift

as those oh so devoted waves

seize and run away with

thoughts and unease

watch them melt away

with the hours

in the sunlit mirror of the sky

you can find me here

slow waltzing with the tide

losing time and troubles

collecting diamonds

from the shore

between my toes....

sand falls
from my crown
like shattered diamonds
on the ground
and the sweet salty
it still lingers
on my lips
my skin blushes
by the burning touch
of midday sun
I beg to stay
you say
you love to be
close to the sea
and so
the sea I'll be
I've been wearing
the ocean all day
for you
won't you
come drown
in me

The September sun
has blessed me
with a burning kiss
straight from her castle
in far north skies
my skin still blushing
from the way
she lingers so
while coastal winds
run fickle fingers
through my tangled
strands of hair
lacing my brow
with grains it's swept
up from a thousand
glittered shores
and my darling sea
he always leaves
a taste
of the sweetest salt
in the corners
of my ever waiting lips
as the foam soaked sand
begs for me to stay
oh if only I could say
in a language
they would know
if they could speak
the rolling waves
the golden rays
I would tell them
that these feet
will never tire
of tracing along
the oceans spine
and if I could
I'd promise them
with all my heart
that I would pay
with all the words of love
that my old soul could bear
and hope they're just enough
to keep the world at bay
if I could stay
I'd give up all my words
and lay my naked soles
along his arch all day...

Sometimes it will get heavy
and it's okay to let it fall
for even the mighty skies open up
to cry every once
                in
                      a
                            while

*Ofcourse
her heart is wild
her soul blazing fire
it had to be so
how else
could she have survived
through the years
of darkness
without her own light
to guide her path
to her own freedom
don't try
to fight her flames
instead let them bellow
and spend your days
in their warmth*

I am here

in flesh and bone
tainted by years
been and gone
they have left their mark
on tissue paper skin
between the cage
that holds my heart
and the hips
that have given
new life and love
sacred passage through
I am here
with some kind of mind
seeking something
not yet known
I make no claim
to have the answers
but I am here for them
just the same
I am here
a stardust soul
catching the glints
inside my palms
I chase the light
with eyes and heart
in hope it might just
lead me home
I am here
and at the same time
utterly unsure
of what that means
but I give my all
to each dear moment
spilling intention
through every breath
whatever the purpose
or the meaning
and whether I find it
or I don't
I have the journey
so for what it's worth

I am here

Do you know
that who she is
runs so much deeper
and further beyond
the heart beating
inside her chest
and the lips that speak
words so sweet
or whisper curses cold
she is more
than what she does
to feed the mouths
of those she loves
and she is not less
if those mouths
are only few
she is an ocean more
than how she looks
more tangled up
than her knotted strands
and earth stained feet
she is much dearer
than her luxe designer heels
and face like art
and while she may be
the object of your affection
make no mistake
she is not yours
or anyone's object
you see that woman
carrying the weight
of her own world
and many others
on graceful shoulders
she does not need
your judgement
and she does not want
your favour
she demands
to be
honestly
and
unapologetically
herself

Well it's fair to say

that if the shoe has fit

then I have worn it

but I can't seem

to wear the same shoes

for too long

for no shoe

I have come across yet

has compared

to the soles

of my dirty feet

when bare

Well I can't spend
too much of my time
ruminating on bridges
already burned
there was never
any other way
I could have learned
I broke my own heart
more than a handful of times
with graceless indifference
passed it around
like a cigarette
and let it burn
hot and slow
between loveless fingers
before being cast away
once again
and once again
I'd let it fall apart
with nothing left
but the pile of ash and shame
slipping through my hands
but as it goes
we are never really broken
the scattered remnants
on the ground
always fall back together
cinder and ember
with time
creating the wildfire
that is
a heart that has lost
but indeed
has loved...

at times I crave

my darker ways
from nights of which
I seldom speak
the ones spent
chasing flames
and broken glass
like a kind of freedom
I could hold
in my palm
my better judgement
traded for just
a handful of hours
unshackled
from the weight
of burdens gathered
along my way
and on those nights
I learned of things
about myself
that in the past
I thought
ought to stay
under the shelter
of the dark
but I'm not one
to hide my scars
at least not anymore

*Oh she earned
every ounce
of peace in her heart
and believe she earned it well
for she had spent
her share of time
cowering in the shadows
of the dark side
of human nature's moon
she had drowned
in the depths
of her own sorrow
her very breath
sucked from her lungs
in the name
of something pretending
to be love
yes she earned
every ounce
of her peace
through and through
when she fought
her way back
from life oppressed
to that next breath*

My soul is home
rightfully owned
by both
darkness and light
they dwell within
sharing this sacred space
my conscience their bed
and my heart their meal
they pass one another
in the halls
grazing bodies
like tangled lovers
casting shadows
of their dance
under the light
of full moons
and they lust for
the others presence
for they know
just as I do
that without one
or the other
neither of them
could be true

I adored you so
like the night adores her moon
you lit up my skies
and I held you on a pedestal
so high
perhaps
too high
it was really only
a matter of time
before you would fall
and when you did
piece by piece
you took it from me
the adoration
that I tried
so desperately
to hold
now nostalgia
my only star
in the nights dark
once again
left grasping my love
for you by a thread
with rope burned hands
because you wouldn't
let me in
when the pedestal
came down

Unveiled
covered only
by slow fading light
I search her
crown to bare
and slender feet
for a lyric to stir
my soul
and while I could sing
my honey glazed songs
along with the melody
of her gentle peaks
and deep loving valleys
these softest of places
were the very least
of her
it was the voice
in her scars unconcealed
the places on her skin
that had been
asked too much of
the begging question
anchored heavy
within the wells
of her eyes
that would inspire me
the very most...

Don't wonder

who I am

if I have changed

from who you knew

and don't believe

that I am lost

and far away

for I am rolling

on the tide

across my days

and over nights

and I will ebb

and flow until

my tides

no more

She is not weak

nor is she helpless

the irony is

she knows very well

deep down

that she does not need you

it is an act of mercy

for you

that she carries on

hauling the weight

of your indifference

a fool will take her for granted

and for the fool

there will be no mercy

when she finally

walks away

And when the warmth of the sun

hit her face that day

it was as though for the first time

because she finally understood

the gift it was

to see the magic

in what we have somehow

come to see

as ordinary....

To be honest

I think I the loving touch

I crave most deeply

is that of my own

tender fingertips

for no hands

have caused me

quite so much suffering

as mine

Be kind to yourself
treat your heart with care
for who else will
if you will not

Blessed is she
who has known deep cuts
on the soles of weary feet
from rocky paths walked
burden heavy
company scarce
thankful is she
who has cowered
in darkness
and shivered in cold
love lost
and hope distant
grateful is she
with scars layered
over worn flesh
and tender limb
for having danced
with sorrow
for the longest of songs
has left her soul
ringing with melodies
of wisdom
that joy
does not teach

do not assume

that because she does not

throw stones

that she does not see

your transgressions

she simply knows

that she too

has laid her head

more than once

in her own glass house

her slender fingers

trace across pages

leaving footprints of her mind

like travel maps

of all the places

her heart has felt

and all the flames

that burned her

still so tender

on the tips

of those gentle things

you can almost feel

their warmth

as though her palm

may cup your cheek

as you let her stories

pull you ever closer

lean into her

and listen

Her crown throws
rebel strands of crimson laced gold
with sunlights blessing
dancing through her rich shades
of dampened earth
see how tenderly they whisper along
the soft skin under her eyes
and gentle pillows of her cheeks
with passing breeze
like a metaphor for the hidden ways
and parts of us we miss
the ones we forget to see
all tangled up in what is easy
what is clear to naked eye
and shallow mind
will you give the love and time
shed some sunlight on your soul
and search among the tousled strands
the countless pieces of yourself
there is so much more of you
to be discovered yet

Offerings of time
she hesitates to decline
knowing these gifts
are neither for sale
nor will they last
for very long
so she collects them
with the dirt
under her nails
and in the salt
of her tears
she lets them draw
themselves in corners
of her eyes
across her waist
she breathes them in
as her nose brushes over
the strands of her child's hair
and though it may
take all her strength
she resists the urge
to wish even the moments
of her deepest grief away
for these blessings
bestowed by time
make up the wonder
that is
a life well lived

*Break me
tear me down
and shatter my heart
until I'm nothing
but sand and dust
then scatter me
onto the rolling winds
of change
sweet as they are
and let them carry me
somewhere away
and when my dust
finally settles
like waves
upon the shore
I'll hold that comfort
for a time
until those winds
take me
once more*

Oh honey
will you please
stop chasing daydreams
of perfection
for what you are
is far more beautiful
than what you'll find
in any dream

Eyes closed
and breathing
short and sweet
not quite full breaths
she counts the stars
behind her eyes
back from a thousand
in her mind
and it's like the sparkle
steals her thoughts
away for a time
and she forgets
about the rush
shooting past
on the outside
of her closed eyes
and her briefly
quiet mind

Breathe

she inhales
with not so much
as a thought
her heart beats
with no need
to be reminded to
the blood in her veins
courses through
all of it's own accord
she is safe
she is free
she is loved
and for all of these things
she is grateful

She spends her days
along that line
between reality
and dreams
she tiptoes
on that slender divide
and with the colours
of her hopes
she paints the gaps
slipped through by most
she makes them
something
beautiful
for
you...

Listening to
my wild things
I tell outside
it's time to hush
as I lean in
to those sweet whispers
from the part of me
that's still
I'm here among
my wild things
letting them crawl
beneath my skin
gathering all
my budding thoughts
that otherwise
would never bloom
I give in to
these wild things
lend them my mind
just as they please
let them turn the soil
of my soul
and plant in me
new seeds
and I adore
my wild things
the way they've sown
into my soul
a love for sky
and earth and sea
and all the wild things
in me....

I have such an affection
for the in between moments...
that's what I like to call them
the ones in between
the ones we remember
the ones that are subtle
unpretentious
almost empty
there is nothing really in them
like a pause between breaths
but oh their calm
so exquisitely mild
is almost an indulgence
like a tepid bath
on a balmy summer afternoon
their discreet tranquility
taking nothing
leaving nothing
lining our days
and filling the spaces
between the memorable
these gentle moments
I adore them so

She tattoos petals
on her skin
like wild flowers
from within
with roots
that bury themselves
far down inside her soul
and they have grown
despite the storms
of love gone bad
and bad gone worse
in spite of drowning
in the torrent of her tears...

they bloom

like flowers of the night
they relish in the dark
and ask for nothing more
than a canopy of stars
and they'll remind her
how she grows
even through unforgiving cold
for she is grounded
in her wildflower soul

Her every breath

chants songs

of gratitude

for the joy

beyond the pain

her heart drums

to her homecoming

and she bleeds poetry

like rain

I won't rush
this breath
I'll let it in
and out slow
and leave those thoughts
of what's to come
lay in wait
a little longer
let all the things
be out of place
a little more
to pick them up
a thousand times a day
becomes tiresome
and all those things
they will be there
when I am ready
when I choose
but right now
it is my spirit
that needs me more
so if I let the dirt
build up
under my nails
and the dust
upon the shelves
who will be hurt
what will be lost
because as far
as I can tell
the only thing
that I could lose
by minding less
and breathing more
is this ever lingering feeling
the cloud that hangs
over my mind
brewing since the day
the world tried
to tell me
just what this life
is meant to be
and what it's supposed
to mean to me...

she just never had

a simple answer

for even the simplest

of questions

which for most

might float weightless

on the surface

before catching

the gentle current

and drifting out of mind

easy as it came

empty notions

they still sunk deep

into the abyss

of her thoughts

settling heavy at the bottom

joining the symphony

of endless conversations

playing over in her mind

*Pour chills
down her aching spine
as you lend your ear
to her heart song
raw and beating
her pulse rhythmic
with yours
as she whispers
from somewhere deeper
than her throat
of all the things
that love
has made her feel
and she'll say
she has never told
a story like this one before
that these words
she had not yet uttered
to another
until she read her thoughts
mirrored in yours
unseen as passing time
but felt like rolling rhyme
and if your courage
finds you willing
and your pride
allows you so
open your mouth
to spill the secret ways
her scars
have made you feel
and you'll have found
the question answered
of how to make love
to a poet*

She found her wildfire within the very flame that burned her....

and she had
this deep longing
a desire to fall
to just let go
and tumble downward
in an endless descent
passing through
waiting hands
that may reach
or try to catch her
it seemed to her
like there might just be
some kind of peace
within the freedom
of forgetting everything
having nothing
but it is the thought
of losing our very breath
causes us to fear
the depths
of open sea
and in the same way
she would not succumb
to her darkest urge
perhaps deep down
she knew
that neither her peace
nor her breath
truly belonged
to her at all

*The steady ache
that old burden
you've carried it
far enough
now make it your magic
call it out by name
expose it
with your pen
your brushstroke
your body
your voice
capture it
and make it something
heart shakingly beautiful
bring them to tears
with the honesty
of your hurt
and watch it crumble
in your hands
what is raw is real
and there is power in it
own your pain
and it will not own you
anymore*

She always carried that weight through

of spoke words picked up

along her way

and what she learned

was that the words

changed their meaning

the further she went

and as their meaning shifted

so too did their their weight

And of this body
this temple
the high priestess is I
keeper
of this heart
guardian
of this soul
and at her feet
I will lay down
all of my love
and heartfelt praise
let every heart beat
be in worship
of each night
and every day
I will cleanse her
of this stain
I will heal
these open wounds
I'll cut her loose
from ties that bind
I'll walk away
I'll take her far
from this ridged path
of self serving ways
serving no one
in the end at all
and when the moon
bows to the day
of her last taste
of breath, of life
I'll bless this earth
with her mortal flesh
once more
before she falls
back into dust
of the stars
where she began....

*I am
a thousand
and one things
behind the veil
of this skin
I am a million more
than what
you'll ever see
like the night sky
has many stars
as does my heart
have countless scars
but with each one
a little more sunlight
bleeds in
and there are cracks
along my wisdom
honest lies
inside my truths
and the most sincere
of hypocrites
I am
but I adore
to find the ways
that I am still
destined to change
and for all I've lost
I'll treasure
what remains*

*She loved anything
made by hand
she had this belief
in energy carried
by things
that love would linger
in the thread
of a hand sewn garment
or embed itself in the clay
of the vase still marked
with the fingers of its maker
and where she could
she vowed to fill her life
and home
with these soul carrying works
created not though disadvantage
of circumstance
but given life
by mindful hands*

I continue find
the loveliest of times
inside small sips
of strawberry gum tea
and the gentle heat
on afternoon breeze
I would bottle this
if I could
I'd keep it close
to be treasured
like diamonds
and gold
because it's precious
you know
this warm
and tender feeling
these sweetest
of sweet moments
that seem to only exist
lingering in between
the very things
that take them from me
what if I threw
them all away
the empty chores
the needless tasks
scattering them
on the wind
and into the sea
I'd let my dear waves
carry them
far from here
far from me
so I'd be left only
with this ever so soft
and gentle mood
I do wonder
if it's possible
that I might ever
live that way
or if this is only
delusional nonsense
made of daydreams
and nonsensical wishes
of this dreamers mind....

A glutton for the bittersweet

addicted to melancholy moods

she craves the ache of a broken heart

desperate for the burn

and she will welcome bloodshot eyes

and give thanks for these tears

for there is nothing

quite like a fresh wound

to inspire a poet

Some pain
touched so far
so very
deeply down
where even
her words
dared not reach

There were days

when she felt it

so intensely

through her delicate bones

the sheer strength

of her connection

as one with all she saw and beyond

there were others

that felt as though

she was grasping at the clouds

as if she could just hold tight

enough

they might lift her spirit

far enough away

from feeling anything at all

petals from the vase
of sunflowers
in the middle of her table fell
and dried in their scattered design
their unpretentious beauty
had such a way that moved her
the charm in the details
of the over looked
caught and lingered
in the corner of her eye
she found it in the erratic trail
of the pothos vine
and in the spill of the crackle
slowly forming in the finish
of her hand glazed mug
she saw it even in the way
the first rays of sunlight
fed through the geometric print
on the curtain
sprawling it across the room
and repainting itself
over the pantry doors
why she was so drawn
to the subtle and obscure
she couldn't tell
but reason plays no role
when it comes to the aesthete
and her art
for just as they were
in their most humble form
these overlooked details
they were her muse....

I speak of empty hands
of holding nothing
as though I've mastered
the very art of letting go
but the truth is
I give my all
trying to hold
these passing moments
clinging to each second
as it ticks past
moulding memories
with my words
as though they may
burst back to life
it's all in vain
like sowing old seeds
in barren ground
and hoping
they might grow
or wishing on
a shooting star
that fell too long ago
I'd love to keep
a steady hand
on all the things
I've grown to love
and all the time
that I have spent
loving them so
but I do believe
there lies the magic
in knowing these things
can never last
that makes them feel
oh so precious
in the first place...

*And with
the gentle mist
of morning
of a new day
poured in
flushing her lungs
it trailed down
from her chest
following the string
of buttons
along the soft cotton
of her dress
landing in the pit
of her stomach
and there it settled
whispering goodbye
to restless
butterflies
and filling her
with the calm
of dawn....*

and I'll ask
for no crutch to lean upon
as I weigh on weakened limbs
blistered and aching
twisted by the path
I have chosen to trace along
instead I relish
the burn
and take delight
in open wounds
spilling my blood
with every fumbled step
I've made
and in the sting
I'll find release
I'll see what's lost
was never mine
to hold at all
but empty hands
are all the better
to write with

Contentment
It's a word
a feeling
I have become
so very fond of
it's that sense of settle
in the soul
the slow and steady breath
found within those not so
elaborate moments
the subtle in between the rush
that deep down warmth
it isn't intense
it's like the first trickle
of sunlight through
the spaces between the leaves
it doesn't overwhelm
it carries through the days
as light as the scent of rain
the sense of belonging
no matter the place
the knowing underneath it all
the understanding
of the peace that comes
with the surrender
of just being...

Tumble slow
spirit dancing through daydreams
of lonely shores
the twisted embrace of the banyan tree
weaving through sun speckled sand
breathe slow
wishing through daydreams
of autumn mornings
eyes closed drink dewy breeze
through tangled strands over salty skin
wonder slow
spirit living through daydreams
of foamy tides
silence rhythmic ticking hands
washing thoughts out of their reach
live slow
spirit waking in daydreams
these quiet hours
eyes open soak light mirrored in the tide
lay easy now daydreaming...

And it's building
like a storm
in the depths
of the place
where both her breath
and thoughts
are birthed
it whirrs
with an electricity
sparked in ways
that cannot be told
only felt
and it causes
the earth under her very feet
to shudder
desperately anticipating
all that she is yet
to do

She has learned
over many nights
spent wilting
with flowers on the wall
to hold herself
by the hand
and take her own
two feet dancing
even when the lights
have dimmed
and the music
faded
for wildflower souls
need no one
to lead them
rather they write
the words
of their own song

I've always been

that all or nothing

kind of soul

I'd rather starve

to death

than live

on the scraps

of a half-hearted

love...

*Wild chai drips
from her lips
some days more spice
than sweet
she bleeds honey
from her open wounds
into your cup
then spills it out
onto these pages
mixed with milky tears
in hope that one day
they might just reach
a needing heart
somewhere out there
that love had once
turned sour*

I like to think

I might be like

a warm brew

of wild chai

with just a touch

of smooth vanilla

and a dash

of sweet spice

blended slow

to my own

kind of perfection

and best enjoyed

under a twilight moon

in pink and lavender skies

and while my taste

may not be

quite your dream

cup of tea

there's no such thing

as pleasing them all

anyway....

And to

that incredible creature

from whom my life

was formed

I cannot say

Thankyou

for how very short

the words fall

when it comes to

expressing the gratitude

from the heart in my chest

to blood in my veins

for eyes that see

and the mouth to speak

the thoughts

from the mind

which would not be

if not for her....

- Mum

Thankful Grateful Blessed

I almost wasn't going to include a gratitude page in this book as I thought it would be utterly impossible for me to fit my praise and thanks for all the blessings I have received in the form of beautiful souls along my journeys way....

But it simply wouldn't be complete without a page dedicated to you all.

So here I want to say *Thankyou*.

To every person who has ever spoken kind, encouraging words in my direction - you may never know how dearly they were needed.

To everyone who lended me a caring ear, advice and guidance when I was out of my depths.

To the incredible creatives that have supported this little dream of mine until it was strong enough to breathe life on its own.

Without naming names, I do hope all of the above know who you are. I certainly do, and hope you know that I can only wish for the opportunity to return the favours tenfold when you need.

Darling

be your own perfect

cup of tea....

Cheriese Francoise Anderson is an Australian poet living in North Queensland.

Drawing much of her inspiration from nature, life experience and her own spiritual journey, she rejects traditional restrictions of poetry in favour of free falling, smooth as honey flow.

"I find writing very therapeutic. One quote about creative writing that has resonated with me comes from Joan Didion - "I don't know what I think until I write it down." I try to let my own writing flow unrestricted, as I find that this is a beautiful way of producing a very raw emotion - and that cannot be forced."

'Wild Chai' is a compilation of her signature soulful odes to both her own feminine energy, and that of women around the world.

If you enjoyed 'Wild Chai' you can follow Cheriese Francoise Poetry on Instagram @ cheriesefrancoisepoet for new poetry weekly, and to be kept up to date on current and future book releases.

www.ingramcontent.com/pod-product-compliance
Lightning Source LLC
Chambersburg PA
CBHW070306010526
44107CB00056B/2508